All the best,
Gila

THE ROADMAP ENDS HERE

ENTERING ADULTHOOD

Gila Daman

ISBN: 978-1-4834-5741-3 (sc)
ISBN: 978-1-4834-5742-0 (e)

Library of Congress Control Number: 2016914139

Lulu Publishing Services rev. date: 8/31/2016

For my father

Contents

Preface ix

Acknowledgments.. xi

Introduction: Will I Ever Be in Kansas Again? xiii

Part I
Gila the Intern:
The Transition from Student to Professional

What Lies Ahead? 1

In the Tests of Life, There is No Partial Credit 3

When Technology Naps...5

Being Cheered On in Life 7

Right-Handed Habit...9

Process Evaluation Versus Outcome Evaluation 11

Are We Energizer Bunnies?.................................... 13

Results from Our Efforts Are Not Immediate:

Lessons from a Soap Dispenser............................... 15

Conflict with Another or Conflict within Ourselves? 16

Nurturing Your Inner Child in Adulthood 18

Broadening One's Vision 20

A Twisted Hose..21

From Frustration to Joy 22

Learning to Trust Intuition 24

Part II
Joining the Ranks of the 9-to-5

Both the Artist and the Art 29
Re-aligning the Body as Well as the Mind 30
It's Not What You Do but How You Do It.............................32
Tomatoes Are Juicy and So Is Life! 33
Pondering Wisdom and Adulthood 34
The Art of Discipline: Endure the Tears (Your Own, Too!) . 35

Part III
Adulthood: Where's the Confetti?

Adulthood: Where's the Confetti? 39
I'm (Not So) Wide Awake! 41
The Good Kind of "Pyramid Scheme".................................43
Daylight Saving Grace 45
Are We Givers or Are We Takers?......................................47
The Challenge of Not Having Challenge............................ 50
Growth Suits Me 52
Just Cruisin' 54
Two Wrongs Don't Make a Write.. 55
No Grace After All: Life Begins Outside of
One's Comfort Zone 57
Part of the Bigger Picture...59

Epilogue...61
About the Author.. 63

Preface

I started writing a year after my father passed away. He died suddenly at the beginning of my senior year of college. That year, I ran harder and lived harder in memory of my dad, an avid runner. The next year, I had to stop running when I pulled a muscle in my leg. That is when I transitioned to "running with my fingers" on my laptop. I was flooded with new thoughts and emotions that I had never experienced. With the loss of my father, I gained access to an inner voice that I had never heard. Or if I had, I hadn't spent much time with it to really get to know it.

During my mid-20s, I often wondered how my life would have been different if my father were still alive. I blamed challenges I was having on my father's sudden passing, on having lost one of my greatest cheerleaders in life. Perhaps I would have made better decisions had he still been rooting for me and guiding me.

After a while, I realized that I would have encountered challenges even if my father were alive, since, at 21, I had just begun the stage of early adulthood. In fact, I was smack in the middle of the period of emerging adulthood, a term coined by Jeffrey Arnett for the ages of 18 to 25, a period of growth and transition that is fraught with challenges. I acknowledged that I would never be able to fully determine which challenges were due to my transition from adolescence to adulthood and which were due to the tragic and sudden passing of my beloved father.

My 20s were a mix of ups and downs. This book is a testament to the ups—to discovering my inner voice and finding faith and clarity. Part I was written when I was a dietetic intern. Part II chronicles my experiences when I began my job as a registered dietitian nutritionist. Part III describes my continued growth and learning. It is my hope that these short pieces will help others as they have helped me: to look at things with a fresh perspective, to find new optimism, or simply to laugh.

Acknowledgments

To my listserv of family and friends. This book began with you. Some of you have been reading my writings for more than five years while others have just recently begun. Each of you has strengthened my belief in what I have to share. Know that each email that you sent with your responses and positive feedback lit me up inside and made me feel supported and connected to a greater good. Thank you for joining and for participating in my listserv.

To my mother-in-law, Miriam Polon, thank you for contributing your editing expertise to this book. It was truly a pleasure to work with you and to spend this quality time.

To my mother, you have been a constant source of positive feedback and insightful critique. Your own journey as a writer, educator, and public speaker has been, and will continue to be, an inspiration for me. Thank you for your unconditional love and support.

To my brother, thank you for being an active participant on my listserv and for being a sounding board for me while I was compiling this book. I very much appreciated your thoughts and perspectives.

To my husband, Isaac, I hesitated to let you read my writings at first, since I cared so much about what you would think. Ever since I showed you my writing, you have been an avid supporter. Thank you for your love, wisdom, and patience throughout the putting together of this book, and always.

To G-d, thank you for the gift of life. Thank you for creating opportunities for growth and healing.

Introduction

Will I Ever Be in Kansas Again?

Emerging into adulthood feels like hearing that your home has been destroyed in a tornado.

You yearn for the comforts and the nurturing of what was, but it's all gone.

You're in the real world now. Deal with it!

Or don't.

But living in your parents' basement is not so pretty either. Staying in your home past a certain age means living in a place you have outgrown. Even if the comforts are there, it isn't healthy to rely on them as heavily as you used to. They are, in essence, gone.

So you go out to forge a new life—to support yourself financially and face the big bad world.

And over time, you create a new version of home.

Instead of your childhood bedroom, you find a place in your heart where you feel safe with your thoughts and feelings.

You learn to recreate your parents' warm embrace by celebrating your big (and little!) victories with positive self-talk and self-appreciation.

Part I

Gila the Intern:
The Transition from
Student to Professional

What Lies Ahead?

Have you ever felt daunted by a future yet untold?

This morning I unintentionally stepped into the front of the first car of the subway. As I looked before me, I saw the tracks forging through the dark alleyway of the subway. My first thought was, "Wow! This is like a Universal Studios ride, and I am in the front seat!" Moments later I realized how truly "wow" this was—but for another, deeper reason.

You see, I was on my way to the first day of a new internship rotation with a nutrition consultant downtown. For the past week, I had been fretting and dreading what was to come: "The hours are going to be so long!" "She is going to assign me so much extra reading!" "I'm going to have to travel to four boroughs in the span of five weeks—and I don't even know which ones!"

My anxiety had gone so far that I neglected (unconsciously, but clearly intentionally) to e-mail my preceptor about my first day until the Saturday night before. "Who waits to e-mail their preceptor until the weekend right before they start?" was my mother's shocked remark.

And while I couldn't give a logical reason, I surely had many irrational ones. Like: Fear. Fear of what was to come. Fear of how little sleep I was going to get. Fear of returning to the structured and scheduled life I had endured in college...

I gathered up my courage and was in good spirits for my first day. And this morning, as I stepped into the front of the subway car and peered out toward the winding tracks before me, it was as if G-d was sending me a message of comfort: "Gila, I understand it is hard to live a life not knowing where each step is taking you and what the future holds. Here, I will let you experience the sheer relief of seeing the inner workings of how and where you are traveling."

Viewing the tracks twisting and turning before me, I felt deep solace. During the ride, I saw another train up ahead. As the red light shone on the tracks notifying the conductor to wait, a part of me wanted to jump up and announce to my fellow passengers, "There is a train up ahead, so we will be delayed a couple of minutes!" The antsy feelings I usually have while waiting in a stalled subway car were completely gone. I felt calm, soothed by the clarity that I had been afforded.

Imagine a life where for every stalled car and unknown twist and turn, we knew exactly what lies ahead causing the blockage. Imagine if we were aware of whatever physical or spiritual forces were delaying the fulfillment of our hopes and dreams. This would eliminate so many feelings of frustration and fear.

Truly, this is a major challenge of being human: having to work so hard to get to where we want to be, yet all the while never really knowing exactly where we are going.

Alas, life is not as transparent as my subway ride this morning. However, this experience allayed my fears and gave me hope that with every step I take I am coming closer to where I want to be; even if the path is unforeseen and I meet obstacles along the way.

In the Tests of Life, There is No Partial Credit

In school, my math teachers said that as long as we showed our work, we could receive some points, even if our final answer was incorrect. This concept resonated with me this morning in another episode of "Academia, why did you train me to be so incompetent?"

I arrived to my internship late because of early morning subway changes and was kindly instructed, "Next time you come late, please call the office and let me know." I explained to my preceptor that I tried calling the office, but I got the wrong extension. My preceptor told me the correct extension and reminded me again to call next time should the same situation arise.

As I insisted again that I had tried, I realized how foolish I sounded. Who cares if I pressed the resend button on some number on my call registry? The fact was that I did not take the time to confirm the exact phone number. Clearly, I should have done this on my first day of the internship.

It is likely that this faux pas was rooted in my being in a state of denial and/or avoidance of my new professional role, but that is a topic for another time.

For now, I want to focus on why I would expect any acknowledgment or kudos for attempting to guess the correct office number. If anything, that was even more embarrassing than completely forgetting to call. I knew how important calling was, but I didn't take the necessary steps to make sure that I was doing it right.

Am I totally clueless and flighty? Perhaps. But I would argue that my experiences as a student contributed to my negligence.

The concept of partial credit in school accustomed me to be complacent when I felt I couldn't do it all. In school, if I knew almost everything else I could miss a couple of points and still get an "A."

This attitude, though it calmed my nerves during an exam, is indeed counterproductive to the tests that life is currently giving me. Missing some points here and there doesn't cut it for my supervisor, it will not cut it for my boss, and it will not lead me toward growth and success. School taught me how to amass knowledge, but not how to succeed as a professional.

When Technology Naps

This Thursday I arrived early to my internship site eager to get a prompt start on the day's tasks. While brewing myself a cup of coffee in the administration office, I turned on the copy machine to copy a research article for a presentation. I entered the department code, ordered five copies, and pressed start.

It must have been at least five minutes later, and still there was no sign of copying action. I checked the machine—lo and behold, the copier was warming up. Two minutes later I checked again. The copier was still warming up. I thought to myself: I woke up near the crack of dawn this morning and this copier is still sleeping!

On the one hand, I could relate. I, drinking my cup of coffee and eating my morning muffin, was also warming up. But on the other hand, I was frustrated with the copier. I pushed myself to wake up bright and early to get a head start on my workday and the copier is still asleep!

Thinking back, this was not my first experience with technology that was slow to warm up. At my last internship site, I remember making copies in the morning and waiting eagerly for the copy machine to perk up and do its job. Not to mention the countless times my laptop turned off or went into sleep mode during a five-minute break from a hectic day of writing research papers.

And then it hit me. The very technologies that we have created to speed up our world are teaching us to slow down!

A tired intern fumbles into the office eager to be productive and efficient and the copy machine gives her a gentle reminder to take it easy. A laptop poops out amidst an overstressed student's frantic paper writing. The laptop is working too hard, so it takes a nap!

We resentfully call it "failing technology," "good-for-nothing," "needs to be upgraded," but there is really a message behind it. One can't work 24/7 at 100% capacity all the time. Sometimes one needs to conserve energy and recharge one's battery—to stop being so achievement-oriented, chill out, and slow down!

Being Cheered On in Life

This morning I got on a different subway than usual to go to a food systems meeting. I knew I was going to be getting off at a special stop—that of Yankee Stadium. As I stepped onto the subway, I soon realized from the mass of people wearing Yankee paraphernalia that there was going to be a Yankee game today.

I took a seat near a father and his young son, who must have been around the age of 7. The father asked a fellow traveler which subway to switch to in order to get to Yankee Stadium. It was likely his first time taking his son to a Yankee game—what a momentous occasion! Both father and son seemed excited as they journeyed on their way.

It turned out it wasn't just the young boy's first game; it was also the opening day of the season! I overheard the father mention that he hoped he and his son would get to Yankee Stadium by noon to see the opening ceremony, where they would distribute the championship rings.

My mind soon returned to the present moment, where I, a dietetic intern, was on my way to a food systems meeting in the Bronx. Time to gear up for another day of expanding my nutrition knowledge and skills.

Walking up the stairs, I passed a subway teller booth with a sign inside that read, "Welcome, enjoy the game!" Signs pointing to Yankee Stadium were everywhere, and spectators abounded. I marveled at the trombonists who were greeting the hordes of Yankee fans entering the stadium.

I thought to myself, wouldn't it be nice if every day we were greeted with such energy and cheer? Any professional deserves a healthy dose of moral support: "You go girl! (Or boy!)" With all the obstacles and stresses of daily tasks and obligations, I could really use some cheering on.

I was grateful that my first food systems meeting coincided with celebration and a parade of excited fans. I hope I can remember the feeling of support and cheer that I experienced that day, and remind myself every day: "Welcome, enjoy the game!"

Right-Handed Habit

For a right-handed person such as myself, the right hand is not only stronger but more adept. It seems to me that it is the adeptness of the dominant hand, rather than its physical strength, which makes us humans feel more powerful in our lives, and consequently less humbled before our Creator. For with habit comes ease of action. And through this ease comes the sense that we humans are the ones creating and developing the world.

In my continuing efforts to act with less force and more faith, I am working on recognizing that the world is unfolding before me, rather than insisting that I am the one calling the shots. But let me tell you—maintaining the realization that I am not in control is hard, because, on the surface, I am! I am the one typing away on the computer. I am the one completing the research assignments.

This past week, I decided to type only with my left hand for a while. After a few minutes of struggling and moving at a snail's pace, I switched back to my right hand so that I would be able to effectively complete my assignments. But I needed only those few moments to remind me that with my own force, I am nearly helpless.

Oh, how our habits veil the true reality! Man may act, but it is only with G-d's help that he can achieve. Perhaps, habits are a test. Are we going to get carried away with how adept we have become? Or are we going to remember that we, too, were once young children practicing how to hold a pencil and write neatly on the dotted lines?

Process Evaluation Versus Outcome Evaluation

I have long recognized how result-oriented I am. I work in a top-down, rather than a bottom-up fashion. When I begin a task, I tell myself what I expect to accomplish and I judge my success based on whether I am able to fully achieve it. This applies to when I have to write a paper, finish an internship project, or complete an assignment for my yoga certification. At the end of the day I am often disappointed when I have not completed every single part of my anticipated tasks.

I continue to work on this aspect of myself. I am trying to have more patience and to be mindful of the present, rather than living my life constantly anticipating the future.

About a year ago, I thought of a metaphor from my research classes that could help me slow my mind down and experience reality more fully. Inspired by an exciting dating relationship that I had recently begun, but simultaneously mindful of the fact that it was all so new and there was still so much more to learn, I told myself: Now is the data collection phase of the relationship; I am not yet up to the analysis and evaluation phase. This kept me from jumping to conclusions about how wonderful a future with that person would be.

Last night, I learned two new research terms that further helped me to live in the moment and be more patient with myself: *process evaluation* and *outcome evaluation*. In process evaluation, one assesses an intervention while it is being implemented. In outcome evaluation, on the other hand, the results of the intervention are analyzed after the program has been completed.

This morning I went about my tasks as if I were performing a process evaluation. I judged my morning based on how calm and comfortable I felt while fulfilling my duties —as if I were in the assessment phase—rather than allowing my usual outcome-oriented self to kick in.

I have a sneaking suspicion that continuing this state of mind will not only enhance the process, but it may even lead to a better, more well-thought-out outcome as well.

Are We Energizer Bunnies?

Remember the Energizer commercial with the pink bunny who kept "going and going and going?" We live in a culture today filled with electronic and technological inventions that are advancing at an exponential rate. It took about 100 years after the start of the industrial revolution for the invention of the car. In the past 20 years, we have progressed from sending emails on a computer to taking a photo on our smartphones and instantly posting it on a variety of social media for all to see.

Humans, like the technologies they use, have become wireless.

Corporate employees often work 10–12-hour days, with twenty minutes for a quick lunch break if they are lucky. It seems nowadays that professionals, like the pink bunny, keep going and going and going.

Granted, we humans have been going cordless ever since we traversed from womb to world, but can we really keep going without "recharging our batteries"?

Man's need to eat and sleep reminds us that we are not self-sufficient, all-powerful beings; that we are not self-running.

Wireless technologies are connected to a power plant, but the cord is not visible. So too, our cord to our life source is not visible either. The question is whether we choose to acknowledge our dependence on our Creator. Or are we fooled by the superficial appearance that we are cordless beings?

Making a blessing on the food we eat is one way we humans can declare that we are indeed not cordless beings. Every time we eat, we are reminded of our mortality. We are not angels, and we certainly are not gods. So let us praise and acknowledge our G-d who blesses us with life.

Results from Our Efforts Are Not Immediate: Lessons from a Soap Dispenser

In an attempt to more fully experience the journey of life and focus less on the end result, this morning, I encountered a cute metaphor in my preceptor's office. You'll never guess, so I'll just tell you. It was the soap. Yup, that's right, the soap taught me how to live in the moment and have faith in the process of life as it unfolds. "How is that?" you ask. I'll tell you...

No soap would come out when I pressed the flap of the dispenser. While waiting for what seemed like forever, I pressed the flap several more times. Still no soap. Seconds later, there was a continuous flow of soap that lasted much longer than anticipated, resulting in the formation of a large glob of soap on the corner of the sink.

After a few frustrating trials, I began to realize that this soap was teaching me a valuable lesson. Many times in life, our efforts do not yield immediate results. We just have to wait. It could be 30 seconds. It could be 30 days. Instead of resorting to feeling frantic or performing an action repetitively, we would attain greater peace of mind by remaining calm and having faith that the soap will, at some point, come out.

Conflict with Another or Conflict within Ourselves?

This morning one of my dietetic preceptors called. She works in a clinic a few blocks from my head preceptor and wanted to follow up with me to make sure that I was completing my assignments on schedule. "Man," I began to grumble inside, "I have been meaning to e-mail certain projects to her for days now. I just needed to check a detail here or there before I sent it. If only she could see that it is on my schedule for today!"

I wanted to sort out these feelings of frustration that were bubbling inside of me. So I sat with them for a moment. I began to think about how my role as an intern is to learn, and the role of my preceptor is to help me stay on track. Why should I be angry with my preceptor for doing her job and for helping me improve in my professional skills?

Then I realized that my frustration with my preceptor was similar to the frustration and resentment I feel when my mother reminds me to do something that I have already set myself to do. "Make sure to work on your resume tonight!" "Don't forget to edit that project…" Surely, this is a mother's role, and truly I am grateful to have someone who cares about my success and well-being so much—but still I am resentful, "I know! I know! Leave me alone!"

With both my preceptor and my mother, I already knew what they were saying was true. In their reminding me, I felt that they thought I was being neglectful, when really I was planning on doing it all along. And that is why it was an even harder pill to swallow.

Nurturing Your Inner Child in Adulthood

I think that adults become jaded with life because they have accumulated so many experiences and because they have become so used to routine, both of which contribute to a decreased sense of curiosity and wonder. Life becomes more and more predictable and less and less exciting.

Think about the sense of fascination that a child has when he identifies a cup for the first time. "Cup!" he exclaims, "Cup!" The cup is not inherently exciting. Many have seen it and many have probably used it before, but for this child the "cup" is brand new. It energizes and excites him.

The more accustomed we become to the ways of the world, the more convinced we are that there is nothing new to discover. But this notion is flawed indeed! No matter how much we have experienced, a new experience is just around the corner, if we would just open our eyes to see the newness and freshness around us.

Another thing that children have more than adults is the attention they receive from others. Not only are children discovering new "cups," but the excitement of their discovery is accentuated by the gleeful response of their parents and others around them. "Yes, cup! Good job!" Unfortunately, parents do not always acknowledge their children and give positive feedback. But when they do, the child's feelings of excitement are validated, further increasing the happiness from his new discovery.

As we become adults, others are often not there to provide us with positive feedback. So how can we maintain our childhood joy? By giving ourselves what we got from others as children. By appreciating our successes and giving ourselves more pats on the back (literally or figuratively). We can also surround ourselves with friends and family who recognize our strengths and remind us of them when we need encouragement. No matter our age, we can maintain the joy of childhood by nurturing our inner child.

Broadening One's Vision

Every moment is packed with potential for deep living and meaningful discoveries.

This morning, I was sitting at my usual table in the cafeteria at my food service internship. The World Cup was taking place in Europe, and they had set up a television for employees to watch during their lunch break.

How much fun! But all I could see, sitting slightly behind the TV screen, was the side of the TV set and the back of it protruding into space.

In life, we don't see how all the details connect to form the bigger picture. We don't know which team is winning. Sometimes, we can't even see in which direction the ball is being kicked.

But even when we can't see the screen at times, we can see the machine working and this gives us hope for the final product.

A Twisted Hose

This past Sunday I went home to spend quality time with my mother and help with some tasks around the house. My visit began with a lengthy catch-up of the previous weekend's activities and the insights that they evoked. After that, I began my first task of the day, which was to help untwist and clean the hose in the backyard.

The first step was to disentangle the hose. That was not as simple as it sounded. In order for the hose to be fully untwisted, not one, but two ends needed to be disentangled. And here's the rub—in order to disentangle my end of the hose, it seemed necessary to tangle my mother's end!

My mother then wisely showed me how to pull my end of the hose through the holder in such a way that her end would remain intact.

A thought came to mind: The hose represents mankind. We all live together, intertwined in a web, a network. Every action I take affects others. My up may be another person's down, and vice versa. Maybe that is why people feel so threatened by each other: Every time one person pulls on their end of the hose, another person feels the tug.

I guess this is one of humanity's challenges: How do we disentangle ourselves in such a way that we are not entangling others?

From Frustration to Joy

The same record has been playing in my head for the past three weeks, and it goes something like this: "Oh man, why can't you get your act together! You have a lot of studying to get done and it is already afternoon! What have you been doing all day?"

And while I have some answers, they pale in the face of the great feat I have set myself: to be as productive as previous experience has told me I can be.

But it is not just my lax studying that I am frustrated about. I am also bothered by the frustration itself. A sort of meta-frustration, I guess. I mean, G-d has blessed me with so much. I have been given so much. How can I walk around with a worried frown? It's just not right.

In dealing with this meta-frustration today, I thought of the following idea that helped me to shift out of negativity and remorse and into positivity and gratitude.

I once learned in a class that if G-d has brought you to something, a challenge, a hurdle in life, He can get you through it. As the saying goes, "G-d never gives you what you can't handle."

So this morning, I thought to myself: "Think of how many successes G-d has already blessed you with." In this case, since I am studying for a national certification exam, I thought of all the coursework that I had successfully completed in the past, all the years of academic exploration my parents had given me.

I said to myself: "At this moment, I am anxious about my upcoming exam and frustrated with my study patterns. But I don't want to wallow in a state of despair, because G-d is blessing me with life at every moment, and that deserves at least a smile!"

I started to hum a tune to myself. I hummed with gratitude for everything that had allowed me to reach this point. I was able to pull myself out of the dumps to where I could see how truly beautiful life is. My heart, no longer stuck on sadness, was singing G-d's praises.

Greed is part of our nature. We get one thing; we want the next. But, in this physical world nothing can ever fully satisfy us. This morning, I caught myself falling into hopelessness and regret. But I chose to focus not on the challenge before me but rather on the blessings that have gotten me to this point. In recognizing how G-d was there for me in the past, I realized He would be there for me in the future.

Learning to Trust Intuition

I resent formulas.

A friend reminded me on the phone yesterday of our high school days when I would review math problems over and over again, even though I pretty much understood them the first time around. I did this because I didn't trust myself to understand the questions, and I wanted to review and memorize every permutation of what the teacher could ask.

As a student, the only way I felt secure was when I knew the exact formula to apply in a situation. How many times on a math or science test did I freeze in horror when my mind went blank? How strongly I yearned for recapturing that magic equation that would show me the way.

Yesterday, I was reviewing formulas for food service equations and I could feel myself falling back into that pattern of having to recall every detail of every example, lest I encounter it on my registered dietitian exam and become befuddled.

But today, on the heels of my conversation with my old friend, I approached my studies differently. I read through sample questions and simply tried to figure out what the questions were asking and the most logical way to go about solving them. And do you know what? I got more than 90% of the questions right. I even got many correct that I had missed the first time around the week before. I had always been instructed to memorize formulas, but here I found myself able to intuit them.

I resent formulas because, while they help me solve the problem at hand, they feed into a greater, more global issue: that of not trusting myself, my ability to make decisions, or my ability to think on the spot.

Yesterday, I re-invited intuition back into my test-taking life. Perhaps a formula will help me, but it's time I started to recognize that I may be more resourceful than I give myself credit for.

Part II

Joining the Ranks
of the 9-to-5

Both the Artist and the Art

This morning, as I rode the bus on the way to work, my words to my mother the night before played back in my mind: "I feel like I am both the artist and the art."

I often envision myself as the protagonist of a movie. And then I wonder, if motion pictures had not been invented, would I have this image in my mind? How could I? And my next thought, "Is modern entertainment diminishing my deep soul-searching journey, simplifying it to a two-hour blockbuster?"

This thought often irks me, but this morning I realized that had movies not existed, I probably would have felt like the main character of a novel.

Well, movie or book, this morning I watched myself from an objective third-person standpoint: A young woman venturing off to the Bronx for another day of work. Growing in independence and wherewithal in the very first job of her career. Gradually she is blossoming into a full-fledged adult, all the while coping with the sudden loss of her father almost five-and-a-half years ago. She is a different person now, working 9 to 5, paying bills, managing her finances, managing her inner world. Her perspective on the world and herself is changing, and so too is her perspective on her father's fatal trauma, as well as the full life he led until the moment it ended.

Suddenly, tears began to flow down my cheeks. "I wish my father were here to see me now," I thought. "I bet he would be proud of me."

Re-aligning the Body as Well as the Mind

When you take a yoga class, the instructor sometimes comes up to you and adjusts your position. You may be feeling 100% aligned, but the instructor will nudge your shoulders or chin, indicating that you were not in fact standing up straight.

This comes as a surprise, since you had felt 100% balanced before the adjustment. In fact, the adjustment makes you feel off-kilter!

In life, we get used to living according to certain constructs. Some of these we create through our own observations of the world. Some of them we are taught.

In recent months, my own constructs have been challenged. Things that I thought of as 100% true, I am realizing are not completely on target. When a friend of mine shares a new view on life that is more in line with objective truth, I feel off-kilter emotionally.

For instance, I used to think that it was obnoxious to ask my supervisor too many questions. However, I have learned that I have every right to ask questions. In fact, a manager may want their employees to ask questions if it will enable them to get the job done right.

Life is about learning and being flexible. We do not know everything and we surely cannot close our minds off from gaining insight from others.

We may have to shift our perspective, and it may feel awkward at first. We may have felt more stable and balanced in our original pose, having compensated in our body for this asymmetry, and it is tempting to stay in this known, comfortable state. However, without being open to change, we cannot grow. Although initially the change will cause us to feel off-balance, over time, with patience and work, we can better align ourselves with truth, and we will stand taller and sturdier because of it.

It's Not What You Do but How You Do It

I was anxious about going to work on Monday. I had several projects I had to get done. Technically they were due in three weeks, but I really wanted to get them off my chest. Last week, I forced myself more than once to sit for three hours straight to work on these projects. I was left overworked and burnt out. By the end of the day, I was miserable and tense.

I was dreading going back to another week of balancing my daily work tasks with these long-term projects that loomed over me. Then I asked myself, "Is it the projects I'm dreading or the way I'm handling them?"

The projects weren't due for three weeks. So, why was I pushing myself so hard? Yes, I wanted to finish them and put them behind me right away, but I could give myself another couple of days. I didn't have to finish it all tomorrow.

And then I realized that what I really wanted to put away and never have to deal with again was not the projects themselves, but rather the tense and frustrated feelings that they evoked in me. "Well, well," I thought to myself, "I am running away from my very own feelings— feelings that could arise at any point in the future, spurred by a whole different project or obligation."

Indeed, I could get these projects off my chest tomorrow morning—not by completing them, but by shifting my approach and treating myself with more patience and tolerance.

Tomatoes Are Juicy and So Is Life!

Just when I thought I was getting some semblance of calm and sanity, my life has been turned upside down again. Professionally and personally, things are so up in the air, so dramatic, so heart-wrenching. I just cannot bear it at times.

This afternoon I was eating a salad. It was take-out, since I have still not figured out how to regularly prepare food ahead of time, amid the chaos that is my life—or the perception of my life.

Anyway, as I was eating my salad, I cut into a grape tomato. Seconds later, there I was, my beautiful professional blouse splattered with tomato juice.

It's scientifically logical: You forcefully cut into a juicy tomato and juice spurts out. Yet, somehow, I had decided to challenge this law of physics.

Amid the frustration and angst of the moment, I thought to myself, "That's life: when you bite into it, you get a little messy!" Oh, how true it is!

Pondering Wisdom and Adulthood

I look across the hall and see a charming four-year-old girl glancing my way. She smiles at me and I smile back. The clinic is full of bright and engaging children. Each time we share eye contact and a smile, I feel rejuvenated and energized.

The typical image of a wise person is one whose hair has turned gray and who has experienced the trials and tribulations of many decades.

Maybe according to that definition I am nowhere near "wise." But what am I when compared to a bright-eyed four-year-old?

Do I only have nutritional information to give over? I have recently crossed into a new stage of life: adulthood. By no means have I mastered adulthood as the silver-haired 80-year-old has, but I have arrived. I am in the midst of bearing new responsibilities and challenges. All the while, I still vividly remember and connect with my childhood.

Perhaps there is a deeper message in the smile the little girl and I share: Having crossed over to the other side, I turn to the child of my youth, and report back: Adulthood is hard. It is scary. But know this, sweet child, it is doable!

The Art of Discipline: Endure the Tears (Your Own, Too!)

This afternoon, after I completed a weekly nutrition education group session, a woman came in with her granddaughter. They had gotten a late start, followed by a difficult commute and had now shown up an hour late for the weekly nutrition and exercise program that I co-lead at the clinic every Tuesday afternoon (I do the nutrition part).

The grandmother was respectful and understanding when I explained that she has to attend the nutrition session in order to be able to participate in the exercise portion (the second part of the program). The granddaughter, a girl of about six, was quite sad and, although I didn't realize it at first, she was disappointed to the point of tears.

As I offered her a consolation fruit (we give fruit out at the group), she thanked me with tears gently rolling down her cheeks. She was such a sweet little girl, with big green eyes and a pretty ponytail of thick reddish, brown hair. I looked at her sadly, and I was close to calling the exercise instructor to see if we could make an exception and allow her to come. All along I was insisting they could not go, so as not to set a precedent for latecomers, but the despair and tears of this sweet little girl were very hard for me to bear.

But I maintained my straight professional stance with them and, apple in hand, off the little girl went with her grandmother.

"At least you got an apple," her grandmother comfortingly said to her.

I had kept myself from giving in to this girl's expression of disappointment (which was clearly sincere and not manipulative—at least, not consciously!), but I was left feeling a void in my gut. I sat still for a few moments in my office and felt the pain of the little girl.

I have never been a fan of discipline. I didn't need it much myself as a child and don't foresee myself being a very good disciplinarian as a parent (G-d willing, at the right time!).

I think it is because I usually feel the emotion of the child and cannot rise above it to the call of duty. I feel I cannot always provide structure for them because I get too caught up in their emotions.

This was one of the first times I did not indulge in the emotional situation, did not rush to comfort, but rather maintained the necessary objectivity and discipline. And I discovered that I was left feeling sad. I had to face the discomfort and sit with it.

It made me realize that this little girl's tears were not so far from my own. I tend to want to avoid difficult emotional situations, and here too, I was trying to avoid seeing and feeling her disappointment and hurt. I wondered whether my feelings were a manifestation of my own inner six-year-old's despair over missed opportunities and disappointments.

Or maybe it was more about tolerating the ups and downs of life. I prefer life to go smoothly, and I like to see the same for others as well. Maybe, though, I sometimes have to learn to be happy with just an apple instead!

Part III

Adulthood: Where's the Confetti?

Adulthood: Where's the Confetti?

Growing up, I received awards and certificates. Success was quantifiable. I had landmarks to look forward to and credentials to work toward.

Life is not the same now. As an adult, I have been going out of my way to reenact the rewards of my childhood by taking additional wellness coaching courses. I have realized that although I often already know the information, what I really want is the feeling of receiving a tangible certificate that quantifies my growth in knowledge and skills.

It's as if I am on an achievement-oriented treadmill and can't get off. Ironically, while pursuing more wellness certificates, my own well-being is declining due to the heightened levels of stress required by these commitments.

When I was a student I was trained to achieve: to garner successes, to get into a good college, then into a good grad school, then to obtain a good job. Now I am at that "good job." But I don't know how to turn off the achievement button and turn on the sustainable well-rounded life—one in which I go to work each day as well as take care of my physical, psychological, and social needs.

Today was one of those days when the monotony of the workaday world was bothering me. Is this really what life is all about? Sustenance? Survival? Stability? I want to learn, to grow, to be stimulated. I was encouraged to do that as a child and as a student. But now as an adult my number one priority seems to be to sustain, survive, support, and maintain a stable rhythm of life.

This afternoon, amid my struggle with the realities of adulthood, I received a phone call from my grad school asking if I could take on a dietetic intern at my job. I had evolved from an intern to an intern preceptor. I not only knew enough to practice but also to teach. I was no longer a shy student. Rather, I was a credible and accomplished professional!

I guess there are still achievements in adulthood, but they're less well-defined. Perhaps they are marked not by a certificate of completion but instead by a natural sequence of events that ever so subtly play out over the course of life. Perhaps the celebrations will be more internal than external. Rather than balloons and confetti falling from the ceiling, as occurred at my college graduation, I can have a feeling of satisfaction in my heart, knowing that I am reliable and resourceful.

I would take confetti and decorated certificates any day. But being a reliable adult has its rewards, too.

I'm (Not So) Wide Awake!

This morning I was sitting next to a rowdy child in the subway. He wasn't terribly rowdy, but in my exhausted and irritable state everything was magnified.

After the third time his adorable little sneaker-bearing foot hit my leg, followed by his tiny school bag jabbing me in the arm, I decided that enough was enough. I was going to get up and change my seat!

It's a free country after all!

Then something interesting happened. The young boy—I would guess he was two or three years old—began reading his father's newspaper. That is, he was attempting to read it. And I couldn't help but listen and watch as he inquisitively asked his father what different parts of the newspaper said. The father was checking his phone at that point, so I decided to pinch-hit. I hope the father approved of my interpretation of the article about a brewery with a photo of a cup of beer next to it. Pointing to the picture, I explained, "It's about a drink in a cup."

While at first I had wanted to shirk off the responsibilities of even sitting next to a squirming child, I began to want to empathize with the burdened father and with the universal burden that parenting entails.

Getting up and out in the morning is hard enough for me, and when I project putting kids into the mix, though I for sure want them, I can't imagine how much more exhausting and challenging it will be.

I could have switched seats this morning, but that would have been winning the battle but losing the war. The fact is, I have to learn how to master, or at least tolerate, going about my morning dazed and confused (and irritable!).

The Good Kind of "Pyramid Scheme"

In my efforts to expand my career in recent years and to make more money, I have come across many pyramid schemes. Sometimes they have been straightforward ones where an organization is luring me to sign up for enrolling others into their scheme with the promise that I will be paid some sort of commission—all I have to do is pay a few hundred dollars to join!

Thankfully, with life experience and the advice of an astute husband, I have learned to recognize such schemes and not get pulled in.

Often I am flooded with feelings of wanting instant success—some extra money, public recognition, or another reward. And it is likely that those pyramid schemes are trying to play off of these emotions.

But there is another sort of pyramid model that is by no means a scheme. That is the one that dates back to ancient Egypt in the times when they were building actual pyramids: "brick by brick," as the saying goes. The same model holds true today—for a house or any other building.

While we may not be building physical edifices, all of us are building our own projects and careers, working one day at a time to nurture our greatest aspirations. As the pyramid schemes teach us, instant success feels amazing, but is likely fake, and perhaps even dangerous.

Today, as we begin the daily grind after the warmth of the holiday season, my wish for all of us is that we lay each of our bricks with confidence and gratitude for the process. Then when the time comes, and hopefully that time will not be too far away, may we revel wholeheartedly in our success!

Daylight Saving Grace

They say that the way you do one thing is how you do everything. That phrase popped into my mind this morning when I was filling out forms to get reimbursed for out-of-network health appointments.

I was feeling kind of hazy because of daylight saving time, and I knew my headspace was not ideal for filling out these forms. But they had been hanging over me for a few weeks already, and I really wanted to polish them off.

Two minutes into my Sunday morning productive time, I found myself in quite a tizzy. "Oh Dang! I just wrote my address in the name section!" I blamed the mistake on my aforementioned time lag, but I also acknowledged to myself that I have never been great at filling out forms.

When I was in first grade, we had to create a poster about ourselves that included some fill-in-the blank questions. In the section about height, I wrote I was "Blue" inches tall. This was then covered up by my teacher with masking tape and the number "44 ½." Years later, the masking tape fell off and I was forced to face my childhood faux pas.

"The way you do one thing is how you do everything."

Just as I do not enjoy following directions when filling out forms, so too I do not like following directions in life. I like to have a general idea of what is wanted and then develop my own methods for how to go about achieving it. I may not stay on point for every specific detail all the time, but the finished product is immaculate and covers all the bases. I need some wiggle room and freedom to do things in a way that is creative and expresses my vision and intentions.

On paper, I may mess up sometimes. But give me a chance to step off the page, and I will soar.

Are We Givers or Are We Takers?

With all the self-help and psychology books that I have read, I have coined a new term, which I call "The Taking Giver."

In this scenario, there are three categories of people: Givers, Takers, and Givers who Take—i.e., Taking Givers.

The "Taking Giver" is one who seeks to get something by giving. Now, this is not to say that the person is selfishly taking. In fact, this process is quite subconscious. What I am referring to is a phenomenon, if you will, that I have discovered within myself.

For example, I write an article for a newsletter and I seek out praise from the readers. I give a presentation, and I crave positive feedback from my audience. I help someone make a job connection and wait with bated breath for them to shower me with gratitude.

I like to help people, I really do. But I also really like the feedback I get when I do it. More than that, I need that positive feedback. And without it, I get quite discouraged.

I experienced the "Taking Giver" mindset again just this past week when I gave a presentation to the medical residents.

I was excited to give my presentation. I had been working on it for two months. I had done a lot of research and put a lot of effort into editing it and making the lesson palatable and effective. Finally, the day arrived. The presentation went from

12 to 1 pm, but my experience of the aftermath lasted much longer.

What did the medical residents think? Did they find the information useful? Did they think my running commentary and jokes were funny? Do they think I'm smart? Do they think I'm funny? Am I a total weirdo?

I was feeling particularly anxious following the presentation and couldn't stop thinking about it all yesterday evening. Why can't the world be a little kinder? Why does positive feedback seem to be thrown out the window in adulthood?

These thoughts continued until today. Then this afternoon, I got the reward I had been searching for. Last week, as a total coincidence, a medical resident informed me that there would be a full-day seminar on the primary topic of my presentation only two days after my own presentation. "Wow," I thought, "this subject is really catching on, and I am part of a new wave!"

I planned to attend the event, but only for the afternoon portion, since I had clinic that morning. I was excited to attend even half of the event, although deep down I wished that I would somehow get to catch some of the morning part as well.

Then, this afternoon, I checked tomorrow morning's schedule and realized that it was much lighter than usual, and in fact, I might be able to make it to the entire full-day seminar after all. Sure enough, after speaking with my clinic co-workers, I found that I would be able to attend the seminar in its entirety.

I raised my arms up in victory with a great big smile! And suddenly I realized that this was my reward for giving that presentation!

Perhaps I couldn't get feedback from most of the medical residents who attended my presentation, but this was bigger than that. This was the universe telling me, "You are on the right track. You worked hard to make a contribution, and now you can attend a seminar which will further your capability to educate on this topic."

In the end, although it took a different form from what I expected, I gained just the affirmation that I was looking for.

The Challenge of Not Having Challenge

Last week, I gave two presentations and attended a full-day seminar based on the topic of one of my presentations.

It was a real doozy! Adrenaline had been pumping through my veins all week and even had begun a few weeks before with the anticipation.

This morning I awoke to a work forecast of "clear skies." The stress was gone!

What a relief! Right?

Well, not quite. While I am happy not to have the pressure of giving presentations, the purpose and meaning that I felt last week are less palpable. The adrenaline in my system is still hanging around in the background of my mind, waiting for a new project to feed its "need for speed."

"But, alas," I explain to my recently revved-up self, "Not every day can be an adventure, and it's healthy to appreciate the calm and routine of life too."

I have tried meditating in the past, and it has helped to slow my mind down and ease me back into the comfort of the now. I will likely try it again at some point today.

In our American society, where there is so much emphasis on achievement and success, we are used to kvetching about how much is on our plate and how over-worked we are. And for good reason!

But getting back into the more mundane swing of things after an extra-busy, project-ridden work spurt is challenging as well.

Counterintuitive? Perhaps. Yet nevertheless true!

So this morning, I raise my water bottle with a toast to the transition from extra-busy to mundane workdays, with the acknowledgment that this transition is not as easy as it may seem.

Growth Suits Me

After a long weekend that was further lengthened by a lingering cold (a real bad one!), I returned to work this week only to be greeted by a string of ten or so emails discussing new procedures that my co-workers and I would be implementing in our daily practice.

One of the great things about gaining experience at one's job is developing routines that save time and energy. Now I would be forced to undergo the typical process of trial and error that comes with starting a new method.

Was it not just a few weeks ago that I celebrated giving a presentation to medical residents? After such a feeling of growth and mastery, why must I return to more humble tasks?

A mentor of mine once told me that growth is not a simple positively sloped curve, but rather one of multiple peaks and valleys which is moving in a general upward direction.

This means that I have not completely fallen off the curve (which is how I feel!), but rather that I am simply in one of the dips of an overall climbing trajectory.

That is somewhat of a relief!

At some point last night, amidst the surprise and frustration of dealing with the new protocol, the idea popped into my mind that I could wear a suit to work; the type of outfit I wore when I started my job five years ago.

Wearing a suit puts me in the mindset of being professional, mindful, and sleek. It keeps me feeling and looking confident when inside I feel bewildered by all that's before me.

Once I thought of the suit-wearing idea, I realized that I didn't have to wear it physically—only mentally: I needed to accept a new challenge to approach my work with greater attention, care, and mindfulness.

Just Cruisin'

Last week my supervisor unleashed some annoying new procedural revisions for me and my co-workers. I am a creature of habit who highly values ease of practice and mastery of routine. Needless to say, these revisions perturbed me.

After a week, I could feel myself slowly acclimating to the changes. The situation seemed to validate what I often find to be the case: Changes—once enacted—are not as bad as I anticipated.

This afternoon, feeling more competent at my new tasks, I found myself attacked yet again by change and by a feeling of being out of control. I somewhat expected it with my job, but with my upcoming vacation!

I was rudely awakened this afternoon to the reality that I had to do even more preparation for my upcoming cruise than I had thought. Apparently, if one does not sign up in advance for day trips away from the ship, they may get sold out and be unavailable that day. And that is in addition to the cruise's multipage online check-in process.

It seems that even to take a vacation one needs to put in a lot of work and effort.

I was so annoyed at all that was demanded of me for this trip that I began to appreciate my job for its relative simplicity.

In that moment, my dream was to take a vacation from all things complicated—including vacations!

Two Wrongs Don't Make a Write

"If you write it like that, you're not gonna fit it in the line."
"This is how you make the loop."
"Let me show you how to do that. That's not how you do it."
"Not a big T. Erase that. The only time you put a capital letter is in the front."

Taking the subway on the way home from work this afternoon, I sat opposite an adorable little girl about five years old who was doing her homework with her father.

I could see the girl really wanted to do it right. She was paying careful attention to her writing and wanted to please her father and do a good job.

Watching her, I was reminded of my experiences in my own childhood with penmanship—or, should I say, the lack thereof.

I wondered if my struggle with negative self-talk began in part due to my less-than-average handwriting as a kid. I remember that in third grade they wanted me to use a triangular grip on my pencil. All I know is that I am darn lucky computers have become so popular. I'm a good typist, and that is all anyone needs to know!

The point is that children tend to personalize their experiences. If mommy is in a bad mood when I come from school, I must have done something wrong. If the teacher says I am a disruptive kid, there must be something inherently wrong with me.

We are so sensitive as kids. That afternoon on the subway, I wondered: What comments about my behaviors did I take to heart that helped form my concept of who I am today?

No Grace After All: Life Begins Outside of One's Comfort Zone

When I was a kid, a science teacher taught us that the primary way to tell that something is alive is if it is moving.

The adult sign of life however is different. We are sedentary after all! But here is the sad and disconcerting truth: How do you know when you are alive as an adult? When you have a headache.

A headache is an indicator that you are awake even when you really, really don't want to be. Besides being a sign of dehydration and/or a hangover, it may also serve as a signal of stress, sleep deprivation and exhaustion—at least that is the case for me.

According to that theory, I am very much alive today—i.e., my head is throbbing.

Even with improved self-discipline about shutting down my laptop last night, I still somehow found a way to go to bed too late. I checked my email before I brushed my teeth, only to come upon a very disturbing message that my out-of-network insurance reimbursement had been mailed to the provider of the services, instead of to the subscriber—i.e., me!

I signed onto my online insurance account, only to confirm my worst fear: In order for me to get reimbursed, I would have to start the process all over again.

Naturally I got myself into quite an anxious tizzy, which I came out of only after I had used up all my capacity to fret and fidget.

At one point, I unreasonably felt that I would live the rest of my life in this aggravating state of powerlessness and confusion. How could I leave this problem unresolved and wait a whole 18 hours before I could contact my insurance company and then the service provider? I had been gearing up for a busy and productive workweek, fighting off jetlag from a recent trip out West—and now this!

Which brings me to this morning. Sure enough, I did fall asleep, albeit two hours later than I had intended. I awoke to a calmer self, still edgy but managing, with a big old headache to keep me company for the day. And off I went to the daily grind.

I know the world will not wait. Things will be unresolved, and I must continue to trudge along. After all, that is what we all must do.

Part of the Bigger Picture

On the bus to work today I had an epiphany. And it wasn't that I should have taken the first bus that came instead of waiting for the second bus, which arrived a minute later— although it was related.

When I saw the second bus coming I decided to wait for it since the first bus was very crowded. To enhance my bus riding experience and therefore my morning, I decided to wait two minutes for this second bus, which was just one block behind.

I began to feel uneasy about my decision when I realized that people were now coming from a later subway to board this second bus. I feared my much-desired space would be gone.

It turned out that the bus was quite spacious and roomy and waiting those two extra minutes paid off.

But there was a point at which I was not too sure. As we were about to board the second bus, an elderly woman with a walker approached the bus. Quelling my instinctive impatience and frustration, I stood right next to the bus ramp as the driver lowered it for the woman to enter the bus.

I watched the ramp carefully; first, because I was standing a bit closer than I intended and was concerned for my own safety, and second, because I was trying to calm my nerves. After all, I wanted to get on with my commute! The ramp moved downward and extended. The woman stepped on it and rose up several feet to the floor of the bus.

I thought to myself that although one strong person could have carried this woman up the steps, this mechanism, built by the joint effort of many individuals, including engineers and mechanics, provided a much more effective and efficient method.

As I started my day, I pondered the role that each of us plays in the bigger picture. Each of us is an integral part of a larger machine, which could not function without our individual contributions. Although we cannot see it in the midst of our day-to-day tasks, all of our actions combine to make a much greater whole.

Epilogue

What Am I?

When I was 19, I decided to become a nutritionist. I had always loved health; since my childhood, my family had inspired me to be health-conscious. I have given nutrition advice to my friends and distributed veggies since I was eight years old. Before I set out to become a nutritionist, I considered being a doctor or psychologist. Nutrition was a combination of health sciences and counseling, so it made perfect sense to me!

All of us go through that period when we decide "what we want to be when we grow up."

But much of what we become is not actually under our control. In life, we will have experiences unrelated to the classroom and our academic or professional aspirations.

If you had asked me when I was 19 whether I would be a good grief counselor, supportive of friends and co-workers who experienced the loss of a parent or other relative, I would have said that I didn't know what you were talking about.

If you had asked me when I was 19 whether I would be giving women's health advice to some of my single friends when I was in my late 20s, I would have been even more surprised.

What am I now?

I am a sensitive person who has experienced a great amount of pain, loss, and heartbreak. Who also has a natural sense of humor and a positive outlook (which thankfully have survived). Who wants to relieve others of their emotional burdens and physical pains. Who wants to give support and a shoulder to lean on and to receive that same support as well.

I am not the person who I thought I would be. And I am not the type of nutritionist that I envisioned myself becoming. In my every interaction with friends, patients, and colleagues, I bring my experiences and my broader, deeper sense of the world.

About the Author

Gila Daman, MS, RDN, CDN, is a registered dietitian nutritionist at a pediatric clinic where she counsels children and their families on how to lead healthier lifestyles. She also presents wellness seminars to clinic staff on topics such as nutrition, mindfulness, stress management, and increasing physical activity in the workplace. Gila obtained her MS in applied physiology and nutrition from Teachers College, Columbia University, where she also completed her dietetic internship. She received her BA in psychology from Brandeis University, graduating Phi Beta Kappa and magna cum laude. Gila is also a certified Pilates mat instructor as well as a certified yoga instructor. Recently married, she lives with her husband in New York City.